BOOKS BY GENEVIÈVE

Merde Encore! 1987
Merde! 1986

MERDE ENCORE!

GENEVIÈVE

Illustrated by
MICHAEL HEATH

"Les beaux gestes" drawings by
ARTHUR FILLOY

F

A FIRESIDE BOOK
Published by Simon & Schuster
New York London Toronto Sydney Tokyo Singapore

F

FIRESIDE
Rockefeller Center
1230 Avenue of the Americas
New York, New York 10020

FIRESIDE and colophon are registered trademarks of
Simon & Schuster Inc.

First Fireside Edition 1995

Manufactured in the United States of America

15   14

Library of Congress Cataloging-in-Publication Data
Geneviève,
    Merde encore!
Text in English and French.
    1. French language—Slang—Glossaries, vocabularies,
etc.   2. French language—Conversation and phrase books—
English.   I. Title.
PC3741.G38   1987   447   87-24123
ISBN: 0-684-81865-5

Aux copains chez Angus & Robertson
(le dirlo Barry et sa nana Cindy,
Murray, Helen, Janet, Roz & Jill),
à mon jules et mes mômes

CONTENTS

INTRODUCTION

Before reading this book, you should have digested or at least nibbled at the contents of its predecessor, *MERDE! The REAL French You Were Never Taught at School*. It's not just that I want you to buy both books ("cela va sans dire"), but I shall at times in this book assume knowledge acquired in the first.

To give newcomers to our linguistic venture a hint of the value of our previous study, think of the importance of possessing "merde" in your vocabulary. People who have changed the course of history have used it, so why should you lose out on such great moments as when Napoleon told Talleyrand, "Vous êtes de la merde dans un bas de soie" (You're shit in silk stockings)? Surely you know of the moment of the word's apotheosis when General Cambronne, having been called upon to surrender at the battle of Waterloo, yelled it out to the British forces, thus immortalizing the five-letter word known ever after as "le mot de Cambronne."

Now, if you enjoyed *MERDE!* and, with it, finally broke the code of those French conversations which had always eluded you, restricted as you were to the French you were fed at school, you will have appreciated the fact that language is not just an accumulation of words but also a key to the spirit and to the character of the people who speak it. You will also, I hope, have had a good laugh in the process. What I offer here is further exploration of colloquial vocabulary and idioms and, through them, deeper insights into the French psyche. French idioms are often very funny, based as they are on concrete and colorful imagery. I'll give you a few examples just to arouse your interest.

Picture this: **"enculer les mouches,"** a priceless image. As you may remember from *MERDE!*, that translates as "to fuck a fly's ass," an image meaning "to nitpick, to split hairs," but how much more colorful than the English translation. So there will be elements of scatology in this book (hurray!), but you must learn to accept that urino-anal imagery, so frequently used by the French, is not necessarily rude. For example, there are two perfectly ordinary and acceptable names for colors which are in the above-mentioned genre:

1. **"couleur caca d'oie"** means literally the color of goose shit yet is a normal description for a yellowish-green hue, and if Zola can use it in his books, why shouldn't it be part of your vocabulary?

2. **"une couleur pisseuse"** (literally, a urinelike color) means a wishy-washy, insipid color.

One more splendid expression, while we're on the subject, to illustrate the concrete nature of many French idioms: **"autant pisser dans un violin"** (literally, one might as well piss in a violin) is used to express frustration, lack of progress, banging one's head against a brick wall. Finally, to show that the visual brilliance of French idioms does not depend merely on excretion: **"sucrer les fraises"** (literally, to sugar the strawberries) describes someone, usually an old person, who has the shakes. Can't you just picture the movement of a hand shaking sideways as it would when sprinkling sugar over strawberries?

I
VERBS:
The nouvelle conjugaison

(Well, not nouvelle to the Frogs, but probably nouvelle to you)

THE MOI-JE SYNDROME

The French like emphasis in speech. This has meant that single pronouns have been found wanting. Therefore, one finds the use of double pronouns, particularly in the first persons singular and plural where this need to underline, allied to French egocentricity and mania for individualism, has given rise to the **moi-je** syndrome:

Moi, j'aime pas ce mec. (I don't like that guy.)

Moi, je suis contre. (I'm against it.)

Moi, je vais te foutre mon poing sur la gueule. (I'm going to punch your face in.)

Special attention needs to be paid to the first person plural, which, you have learned, is "nous." So it still is, but it has been subverted by the now ubiquitous "on," which has graduated from being the indefinite third person singular pronoun ("on dit que" = it is said that) to being the second half of the double pronoun, "nous, on." Worse, the agreement of participle or adjective is with the first person plural, even if "nous" is left out and the verb itself is in the third person singular:

Nous, on est dégoûtés. (We're disgusted.)

Avec les copains, on est allés au cinoche. (We went to the flicks with some pals.)

Disgusting, say the grammar purists! (Mr. Grammar Purist, ever heard of the ostrich or the dodo?)

So, for a final look, an example for each pronoun:

Moi, je suis belle, intelligente et cultivée. (I'm pretty, intelligent and cultured.)

Toi, t'es un pauvre con. (You're a pathetic idiot.)

Elle, elle est moche comme un pou. (She's very ugly, as ugly as sin; she's a dog.)

Nous, on en a marre. (We're fed up.)

Vous, vous êtes des emmerdeurs. (You're all pains in the ass.)

Eux, ils sont débiles. (They're idiots, they're stupid.)

CODE CONJUGATIONS

To make patronizing jokes about clodhopping peasants or Africans as they often do, to their great amusement, the French have "code" conjugations of which you should be aware, otherwise you'll miss the reference (try reading *Tintin au Congo* without such knowledge). The joke-peasant says "j'avions," "j'étions," and "je vas" and is prone to answering a question with "'têt ben qu'oui, 'têt ben qu'non" (in other words, "peut-être bien que oui, peut-être bien que non" = maybe yes, maybe no; maybe it is, maybe it isn't). Meanwhile, in "petit nègre" (pidgin French), the first person singular is "moi y'en a" plus an infinitive, as in "moi y'en a vouloir" (I want); "moi y'en a pas être" (I'm not). The articles "le" and "la" become "li," and "monsieur" becomes "missié." Hence, one could have "Missié Tintin, moi y'en a pas avoir vu li chien Milou" (I haven't seen your dog Milou, Mr. Tintin), or "moi y'en a vouloir toi donner fusil" (I want you to give me the rifle).

II
SUFFIXES:
Instruments of contempt and belittlement

So you think that suffixes are just another boring little grammatical item? Not in French, where some are invested with great power. The French, with their superiority complex, make much use of suffixes to express contempt and belittlement. Here are the basic ones, with a few examples of each (and once you have mastered them, you can coin your own words).

For belittling, meet monsieur −(a)illon:

un avocaillon (from "avocat" = lawyer)   a small-town lawyer

un curaillon (from "curé" = priest)   a village priest

un moinillon (from "moine" = monk)   an inconsequential monk

un criticaillon (from "cri-tique" = critic—literary, artistic, etc.)	a two-bit critic
un écrivaillon (from "écri-vain" = writer)	a hack writer

Meet his many offspring: −(a)iller, −(a)illerie, −(a)illeur:

discutailler (from "discu-ter" = to discuss)	to quibble
la politicaillerie (from "la politique" = politics)	petty politics
un rimailleur (from "rime" = rhyme)	a poetaster

Meet monsieur −ton:

un chèqueton (from "chèque" = check)	a check
un naveton (from "un navet" = a third-rate work of art)	a third-rate work of art
un cureton (from "curé" = parish priest)	a village priest

For contempt, meet monsieur −ard and madame −arde:

un(e) banlieusard(e) (from "la banlieue" = the suburbs)	a suburbanite
snobinard(e) (from "snob")	snooty
un politicard	a politico
froussard(e) (from "la frousse" = fear)	yellow-bellied, scaredy-cat

6

un(e) soulard(e) (from "soûl = drunk) **un(e) soiffard(e)** (from "soif" = thirst)	a lush, drunk, boozer
un(e) fêtard(e) (from "la fête" = a good time)	a hell-raiser
un(e) bondieusard(e) (from "le bon Dieu" = God)	an excessively, narrow-mindedly pious person

For underlining a point, meet monsieur et madame **–issime,** who can be used to emphasize positive as well as negative qualities, depending on what they are tagged on to:

nullissime (from "nul")	totally useless, worthless
gravissime (from "grave")	extremely serious
rarissime (from "rare")	very rare
richissime (from "riche")	phenomenally rich, loaded

III
LES BEAUX GESTES:
French sign language

Platitude: the French gesticulate when they speak. Revelation: they are not always just flapping around; some gestures are a language of their own and need translation. Be very attentive and practice in front of your mirror. (All instructions are given for right-handers; left-handers should adapt them accordingly.)

1. Va te faire foutre!
The king of gestures, known as "le bras d'honneur" (literally, gesture of esteem, respect, homage—a supreme irony). Absolutely vital in all situations, especially when driving.

Meaning: Get stuffed! Up yours! Fuck you!
Method: Right arm stretched out, smack your left hand palm down on the right arm, just above the elbow, making the forearm spring sharply upwards.

2. J'en ai ras le bol.

Meaning: I've had it up to here, I'm fed up.

Method: Using your right hand, palm facing downward, trace a quick line from left to right, level with your eyebrows or across the top of your head.

3. Quelle barbe! Qu'est-ce qu'il/elle est rasoir!

Meaning: What a bore, what a drag! What a bore he/she is!

Method: Loosely bend the fingers of your right hand, then stroke your right cheek up and down with the back of your fingers, between the first and second joints.

4. Barrons-nous!

Meaning: Let's get the hell out of here!

Method: Both hands flat, palms facing downward, smack the back of the right hand with the left palm.

9

5. Y'a quelqu'un qui a un verre dans le nez!

Meaning: Someone's had too much to drink!

Method: Form an "o" with the fingers of your right hand, making a very loose fist. Put it in front of your nose, facing straight ahead, and make a turning, screwing motion right to left (90 degrees will do).

6. Mon oeil!

Meaning: My eye! My foot!

Method: Pull the skin below your right eye downward, using only your right index finger.

7. Aïe, aïe, aïe, aïe, aïe!

Meaning: Uh oh, someone's in trouble!

Method: Right hand palm facing your chest, fingers apart, shake it loosely up and down.

10

8. C'est pas donné!

Meaning: It ain't cheap, it'll cost you.

Method: Right hand palm facing upward, straighten fingers upward and rub thumb up and down the top of the other grouped fingers.

9. J'm'en fous!

Meaning: I don't give a damn!

Method: Right hand out, palm facing upward, make a hitting motion toward your shoulder.

10. Alors, là!

Meaning:

1. I really don't know.
2. I doubt it can be done.

    Method: Raise both hands toward your shoulders, palms outward. Lower lip should protrude and eyebrows rise.

11. Cocu! (An overworked and much favored insult.)
Meaning: Cuckold!
Method: Stick your two index fingers up on either side of your head, like horns, and wiggle them up and down (horns being the traditional symbol of the cuckold).

12. Au poil! Super! Fantastique!
Meaning: Great! Terrif! and so on.
Method: Makes a "thumbs up" sign with your right hand, and stamp it down slightly in front of you.

Note that the gesture of thumbing one's nose at someone is called **"faire le pied de nez à quelqu'un"** or **"faire la nique à quelqu'un."**

IV
GUILLOTINED FRENCH:
From aristo to socialo

Read the following:

Napo détestait les intellos.
Le sous-off est complètement parano.
C'est l'intox à coup de gégène.
Le PDG adore la BD.
À la manif, y'avait beaucoup d'écolos rachos.

Mysterious? Well, the clues will appear shortly. Someone who has been guillotined is said in French to have been "rac-courci(e)," that is, shortened. This is what happens to many French words. The guillotine effect is widespread in conversation and in media vocabulary. It is most often found in words that have, in their original form, an interior "o" (usually in the penultimate or ante-penultimate syllable), that "o" becoming the last letter of the guillotined word. Learn five words a day.

un(e) écolo (écologiste)   an ecologist (à la Green-
                                      peace or the Green
                                      movement)

un(e) collabo (collaborateur, —trice)	a collaborator (the French World War II version)
folko (folklorique)	quaint, out-of-date, folksy
rétro (rétrograde)	said of someone or something that indulges in nostalgia, is old-fashioned, or imitates a style of the past ("**une mode rétro**," "**une politique rétro**")
maso (masochiste)	masochistic
porno (pornographique)	porno
un(e) aristo (aristocrate)	an aristocrat
une diapo (diapositive)	a slide, a transparency (photography)
le croco (crocodile)	crocodile leather, as in "**un sac en croco**" = a crocodile-skin bag
une leçon de géo (géographie)	a geography lesson
un labo (laboratoire)	a lab
un mélo (mélodrame)	a dramatic scene, as in "**faire tout un mélo**" = to act up, to make a big scene
un chrono (chronomètre)	a stopwatch
parano (paranoïaque)	paranoid

14

un(e) toxico (toxicomane)	a drug addict
mégalo (mégalomane)	megalomaniac (a common French trait)
l'édito (m.) (l'éditorial)	the editorial
la météo (les prévisions météorologiques)	the weather forecast

Many words just have the "o" added to their shortened state:

un(e) intello (intellectuel, –le)	an intellectual
un(e) socialo (socialiste)	a socialist
un(e) facho (fasciste)	a fascist
un(e) coco (communiste)	a commie
un(e) prolo (prolétaire)	a prole
un dico (dictionnaire)	a dictionary
un(e) invalo (invalide)	an invalid
racho (rachitique = literally, suffering from rickets)	skinny, scrawny
le, la proprio (propriétaire)	the landlord, landlady
le frigo (frigidaire)	the fridge

Or else they are simply left in their guillotined condition:

réac (réactionnaire)	reactionary

la fac (faculté)	the university faculty
le bac (baccalauréat)	the baccalaureate
la rédac (rédaction)	the essay (a school assignment)
l'occase (occasion)	the opportunity
la pub (publicité)	advertising, the advertisement
le bénef (bénéfice)	the profit
la manif (manifestation)	the demo
un trav (travelot, travesti)	a transvestite, drag queen
un(e) mac (un maquereau/ une maquerelle)	a pimp/a madam
cap (capable)	able (**"T'es cap de le faire?"** = Do you dare do it? Do you think you can do it?)
l'alu(m). (aluminium)	aluminum
un macchab (macchabée)	a stiff (corpse)
le Boul'Mich (Boulevard St. Michel)	(that street in the heart of the Latin Quarter)
le sous-off (sous-officier)	the NCO (noncommissioned officer)

16

l'intox (intoxication)	brainwashing
le, la dirlo (directeur, directrice)	the director (the boss)
le gégène (général)	the general (army officer)
la gégène (génératrice)	torture by electric shock (do not confuse with the above *"le gégène"*)
le PDG (Président-Directeur-Général)	the boss of a company
la BD (bande dessinée)	the comic strip

A special note on "la BD": this is a new art form to which much time, discussion, cogitation, and ink are devoted. It is a thriving industry, and there is even an annual BD festival at Angoulême. To you and me, it is just a comic strip but, as it exists in France, where things must be given a more serious—dare I say intellectualized—bent, it is a boom industry—whoops, art form. French children hardly seem to read books anymore unless they are in BD form, and adults have their own, including porno ones, for their delectation.

Translation of introductory sentences:

Napoleon hated intellectuals.

The NCO is absolutely paranoid.

It's brainwashing by electric torture.

The boss is crazy about comic strips.

The demo was full of scrawny ecology types.

V
COUNTING IN FRENCH:
Some numbers are more equal than others

*"Je n'étais qu'un zéro qui, en chiffre, signifie
quelque chose quand il y a un nombre devant lui."*

Cardinal de Richelieu
*(the number before his zero
being Louis XIII)*

UN, DEUX, TROIS . . .

Some numbers are more favored than others in French, as they are part of commonly used idioms. Before you are introduced to them, learn these few colloquial words for things often counted.

les berges (f.)
les piges (f.)

years, as in **"C'est un vieux gaga, il a eu quarante piges hier."** = He's an old geezer; he was forty yesterday.

les bornes (f.)

kilometers, as in **"J'ai roulé cent bornes."** = I drove a hundred kilometers.

les balles (f.)	francs, as in **"File-moi quinze balles."** = Give me fifteen francs.

Zero is very important, as it quantifies, in the usual negative French way, one's esteem for someone or the level of an activity. We'll start on the other side of zero and move up from there:

c'est un minus	he/she is a nitwit
il est nul **elle est nulle** **c'est une nullité**	he/she is useless, stupid
il/elle est nullissime	he/she is totally useless, stupid
c'est un zéro	he/she is a nothing, a complete nonentity
alors, là, c'est zéro pour la question!	no way, certainly not!
avoir le moral à zéro	to be depressed, to be down in the dumps
s'en foutre de quart comme du tiers	not to give a damn
à un/deux doigt(s) de . . .	on the verge of, as in **"à deux doigts de la mort"** = at death's door
en moins de deux	very quickly

en deux temps trois mouvements **en deux coups de cuiller à pot**	in two shakes of a lamb's tail
se retrouver/tomber les quatre fers en l'air	to fall flat on one's back (the image is that of the horse on its back with its shoes ["fers"] up in the air)
un de ces quatre (matins)	one of these days
tiré(e) à quatre épingles	dressed to the nines
faire ses quatre volontés	to do as one pleases, without taking others into account
ne pas y aller par quatre chemins	to get straight to the point, not to beat around the bush
se plier en quatre pour quelqu'un	to put oneself out for someone, bend over backward for someone
couper les cheveux en quatre	to split hairs, nitpick
dire ses quatre vérités à quelqu'un	to give someone a piece of one's mind

20

ne pas casser quatre pattes à un canard	to be not worth writing home about, to be unexciting (literally, not to break the four legs of a duck)
il y avait quatre pelés et un tondu	there was only a handful of people there (literally, there were only four baldies and one short-back-and-sides)
les cinq lettres	euphemism for "merde"
en cinq sec	very fast, in a jiffy
le mouton à cinq pattes	the impossible, the unattainable
vingt-deux, voilà les flics!	look out, here come the cops!
se mettre sur son trente et un	to wear one's Sunday best
voir trente-six chandelles	to see stars (literally, to see thirty-six candles, after being punched, for example)
je m'en fous comme de l'an quarante	I don't give a damn (literally, I don't care about it any more than I do the year 40)
un soixante-neuf	a "soixante-neuf" (*that* 69, you know!!!)

faire les cent pas	to pace up and down
s'emmerder à cent francs de l'heure	to be bored to tears
attendre cent sept ans	to have a long wait

VOIR TRENTE-SIX CHANDELLES = TO SEE STARS

faire les quatre cents coups	to get into lots of trouble, to lead a dissipated life
je te/vous le donne en mille	you'll never guess

THE FROGCLOCK

In the seventies, a marvelous slogan was coined that summed up the drudgery and routine of the Parisian worker's life: **"métro-boulot-dodo"** (remember from *MERDE!* that "boulot" means work or job, and "dodo" is baby talk for sleep: "métro" [the subway] is the form of transport used daily to get to work). By setting out the daily routine we get the Frogclock:

7:00 café;	2:00 boulot;
7:15 caca et un brin de toilette;	(5:00–7:00 baise);
	7:00 métro;
8:00 métro;	8:00 bouffe et télé;
8:30 boulot;	(11:00 baise);
Noon bouffe;	Midnight dodo.

A quick reminder that "caca" = crap (baby talk but used by adults too), that "bouffe" = grub, food. What's the "brin de toilette"? Nothing to do with "caca"; it means a quick wash (and, in France, that *means* quick . . . see chapter VIII). What about this "baise" (screw) twice a day? The expression **"faire un petit cinq-à-sept"** refers to adulterous sex enjoyed between the end of office hours and the return to the conjugal domain, where marital sex can be had at the later hour. Speaking of fornication, you should know that **"un baise-en-ville"** is a woman's overnight bag owing its name to its original purpose: to contain the necessary items for an illicit quickie in town in the days when contraception required bulkier items than the odd pill. Variation for the young male adolescent: subtract the "baise" and add a 6:30 "branle" (masturbate), replace "boulot" with "bahut" (school) and add another "branle" before "dodo."

A few other times should be noted, as they appear in idioms:

faire passer un mauvais quart d'heure à quelqu'un	to give someone a rough time (literally, to make someone go through a rough fifteen minutes)
les trois quarts du temps	most of the time
un bouillon d'onze heures	a poisoned drink
chercher midi à quatorze heures	to complicate things unnecessarily

Apply your knowledge:

1. Si Lucrèce Borgia en avait marre de quelqu'un, elle ne cherchait pas midi à quatorze heures; elle lui filait un bouillon d'onze heures et en deux temps trois mouvements son compte était fait.

2. Le concert ne cassait pas quatre pattes à un canard; d'ailleurs il n'y avait que quatre pelés et un tondu.

3. Il est tellement nullissime qu'il faut attendre cent sept ans pour qu'il finisse le boulot qu'un autre ferait en cinq sec.

1. If Lucrezia Borgia got fed up with someone, she didn't make a big deal out of it; she just slipped him/her a poisoned drink and in no time at all his/her number was up.

2. The concert was nothing to write home about; anyway there was hardly a soul there.

3. He is so totally useless that it takes him forever to finish a job that someone else would do in no time at all.

24

VI
SOUND EFFECTS:
Gurgle, splash, hiccup!

You don't imagine that the French go "ah-choo" or say "wow," do you? The latter is almost a physical impossibility for them, the letter "w" not really being French (there are very few words starting with "w" in French dictionaries and they are mostly taken from English). To approximate the "wow" sound, it has had to be transcribed as "ouaouh" or, left to its own devices, it would have come out as "vov." Anyway, if you want to understand conversation or liven up your own narrative, you'd do well to learn the following vital sounds.

achoum!	ah-choo
glouglou	gurgle, glug glug
badaboum!	
patatras!	crash!

flac!	splash!
plouf!	
ouf!	phew!
pouah!	poo! (What a stink!)
miam miam!	yum yum!
toc-toc-toc!	knock-knock-knock!
aïe! ouille!	ow! ouch!
heu, euh	um
ben	
boum!	bang!
pan pan!	bang-bang! (gunshot)
clac!	smack!
hi, hi	boo-hoo
youpi!	hurray, goody!
taratata!	rubbish, crap
oh là là là là!	uh oh, oh dear! boy oh boy!
patati patata	blah blah blah; yakety-yak
pinpon	siren of a police car, ambulance or fire engine
hic!	hiccup!
guili guili	(the noise the Frog makes when tickling someone)
bôf!	(a sound to accompany the shrugging of shoulders to show indecision, indifference or ignorance)

There are certain important nouns and adjectives derived from onomatopoeia:

gnangnan (adj.) wimpish and given to whining (from the whining sound)

olé olé (adj.) forward in manner and/or speech; used disapprovingly of such conduct in a young woman ("**Elle est plutôt olé olé, ta copine.**" = Your girlfriend comes on pretty strong.)

un scrogneugneu an old grouch (from the grumbling, grouchy sounds he supposedly emits)

le crincrin the squeaky, scraping sound of a badly played instrument, particularly a stringed one

le tralala the frills, the trimmings

faire du tralala to make a big fuss (when having people over, for example)

les chichis fuss, ceremony ("**Arrête de faire des chichis.**" = Stop making such a big deal of it.)

chichiteux, chichiteuse   affected, lacking in simplicity

A special mention must go to the onomatopoeic **"crac!"** Apart from its sound effect (crack!), the French use it to introduce a dramatic event in a narrative. It is a tool used to emphasize and dramatize. Just before relating the climax of the event, pause, then insert a strong "crac!" and continue your description. Study the following examples.

> **Ils étaient richissimes et, crac! ils ont tout perdu.**
> (They were loaded and suddenly they lost everything.)

Ç'avait l'air de bien marcher et puis, crac! on l'a foutu à la porte. (Everything seemed to be going well and then, suddenly, he was kicked out.)

Il me parlait de choses et d'autres et, crac! il m'a embrassée. (He was talking about one thing and another and suddenly he kissed me.)

A few more sentences to test your general ability:

1. Badaboum! Elle tombe! "Aïe, ouille! Hi, hi!" elle se met à pleurer. Un scrogneugneu qui passe lui gueule: "Vous êtes bien gnangnan, vous!"

2. Toc-toc-toc! "Qui c'est?" "C'est la concierge. Faut arrêter votre horrible crincrin, y'a les voisins qui rouspètent."

3. Miam, miam, des frites!

1. Crash! She falls! "Ow, ouch! Boo-hoo!," she starts crying. An old grouch passing by yells at her, "What a little whiner you are!"

2. Knock-knock-knock! "Who is it?" "It's the concierge. Stop scratching that awful fiddle, the neighbors are complaining."

3. Yummy, French fries!

VII
THE MOST POPULAR INGREDIENTS OF FRENCH IDIOMS:
Food and animals

"Dis-moi ce que tu manges, je te dirai ce que tu es."

A. Brillat-Savarin
(famous gastronome, 1755–1826)

YUM YUM, DRIBBLE DRIBBLE

Here is an appetizer (translations at the end of this section):

1. Oh, dis, hé, arrête d'en faire tout un fromage.

2. C'est pas de la tarte de serrer la cuiller à la viocque: elle sucre les fraises.

3. Alors, mon petit chou, t'es pas dans ton assiette?

4. Occupe-toi de tes oignons, espèce de gros lard.

5. Alors, comme ça, j'ai fait tout ce boulot pour des prunes? La prochaine fois, t'iras te faire cuire un oeuf.

Take a nation of predominantly peasant origin where food has a near-religious dimension, and you are bound to find many idioms based on food imagery, and entertaining they are too. That not very noble vegetable, the cabbage, appears in a number of them, so that's where we'll start.

aller planter ses choux	to retire to the country
entrer dans le chou de quelqu'un	1. to hit someone 2. to knock into, collide with someone
oreilles en feuille de chou	cauliflower ears
bête comme chou	really stupid
être dans les choux	to be in trouble, to be in an awkward situation
faire chou blanc	to fail completely, to draw a blank
chou, choute	cute
mon chou, ma choute	sweetie ("mon chou" can be used for men or women)
avoir du sang de navet	to be spineless, cowardly (literally, to have the blood of a turnip)
les carottes sont cuites	it's all over, all's lost
ne pas avoir un radis	to be broke

avoir un coeur d'arti- chaut	to be fickle, to fall in and out of love easily, to flirt with everyone one meets
occupe-toi de tes oignons!	mind your own business!
en rang d'oignon	lined up in order of height
le panier à salade	the police van, the paddy wagon
une gourde	a clumsy person
c'est la fin des haricots	it's the last straw
en avoir gros sur la pa- tate	to have a heavy heart about something (une patate = a spud)
une grosse légume	a big wheel, a bigwig
la fraise	the mug (face)
ramener sa fraise	to butt in
sucrer les fraises	to have the shakes
des prunes!	no way!
faire quelque chose pour des prunes	to do something for noth- ing (i.e. for no reward or without result)
une poire	a sucker, a mug
couper la poire en deux	to meet halfway, to make equal concessions

les bananes	medals, decorations (military)
haut(e) comme trois pommes	tiny (to describe a person)
tomber dans les pommes	to faint
va te faire cuire un oeuf!	go to hell!
quel oeuf!	what a jerk, what a blockhead!
une andouille	a stupid person ("andouille" is a sausage made from chitterlings)
un boudin	a dumpy woman ("boudin" = blood sausage)
ne pas les attacher avec des saucisses ("les" = ses chiens)	to be stingy (literally, not to tie them [one's dogs] up with sausages)
mettre du beurre sur les épinards	to become financially more comfortable, as in "ça mettra du beurre sur les épinards" = that'll make life easier
discuter le bout de gras	to chew the fat, to gab
en faire tout un fromage	to make a big deal out of nothing
défendre son bifteck	to stand up for one's financial interests

être chocolat	to be thwarted, frustrated
casser du sucre sur le dos de quelqu'un	to say things behind someone's back, to badmouth someone
cheveux poivre et sel	salt-and-pepper hair (often used for a distinguished-looking hue)
mettre son grain de sel	to interfere, stick one's two cents in
salé(e)	1. spicy, risqué 2. dirty (of a story, of someone's actions or jokes, etc.)
ça ne manque pas de sel	it's spicy (as above)
un riz-pain-sel	a serviceman (especially an officer) in charge of supplies, a quartermaster
tourner au vinaigre	to go sour (a relationship, for example)
la sauce	torrential rain
la purée de pois	pea-souper (fog)
un gros plein de soupe	a fatso, tub of lard
s'amener comme un cheveu sur la soupe	to come along at an inopportune moment; to be irrelevant (a comment, for example)

être soupe au lait	to have a short temper, to blow one's fuse easily
gratiné(e)	outrageous, extraordinary (actions, stories)
le gratin	the upper crust
c'est du gâteau c'est de la tarte	it's a cinch, it's easy, it's in the bag, it's a piece of cake
c'est pas du gâteau c'est pas de la tarte	it's a tough one, it's going to be rough
tarte (adj.)	silly and ridiculous (describing people or objects, not events)
avoir du pain sur la planche	to have a lot of work ahead, to have a lot on one's plate
se vendre comme des petits pains	to sell like hot cakes
mijoter quelque chose	to cook up something (mischief, a plot, a deal, etc.)
c'est du tout cuit	it's a cinch, it's in the bag
c'est du réchauffé	it's a rehash, it's stale (jokes, arguments, ideas, etc.)
un(e) dur(e) à cuire	a tough, hard person

qu'est-ce que c'est que cette cuisine?	what's all this monkey business?
bouffer (du curé, du politicien, de l'Anglais, etc.)	to hate (priests, politicians, the English, etc.)
bouffer à tous les râteliers	to be a sponger, to cash in on all sides ("râteliers" = dentures, so literally, "to eat from all dentures")
un pique-assiette	a scrounger, a sponger
ne pas être dans son assiette	to be out of sorts (literally, not to be in one's plate)
en faire tout un plat	to make a big production out of something
se serrer la cuiller	to shake hands (literally, to shake each other's spoon—well, remember that in olden days the hand was the eating utensil)
être à ramasser à la petite cuiller	to be in a pathetic state; to be knocked out (a person) (literally, to be in such a state that one can be scooped up with a spoon)
ne pas y aller avec le dos de la cuiller	to act without restraint, to lay it on thick

36

il/elle n'a pas inventé le   he/she is not very bright
fil à couper le beurre

Translations of the introductory sentences:

1. Hey, stop making such a big deal out of it.

2. It's not easy to shake hands with the old bag; she's got the shakes.

3. What's the matter, honey, are you out of sorts?

4. Mind your own business, fatso.

5. You mean I did all that work for nothing? Next time you can go to hell.

THAT YUKKY FRENCH FOOD

The French could put you off your food, you know! I'm not just referring to the fact that they eat those frogs' legs (some 200,000,000 frogs are imported for consumption a year), snails (40,000 *tons* eaten a year), calves' brains, and so on, it's the names they sometimes use. If you were given the following menu in a restaurant, you might justifiably feel an urge to go somewhere else. However, what you are about to read are literal translations of perfectly acceptable—indeed, highly appreciated—French comestibles.

MENU DU JOUR
Dribbling-spittle Omelette
Piss-in-bed Salad
Choice of Cheese
(Droppings or The Stinker of Lille)
Nun's Farts
(With Ass-scratcher Jam)
Wine: Pissing Hard

O.K., an explanation is coming! In French, the above items would be as follows (and no Frenchman would bat an eyelid):

Omelette Baveuse

Yes, "baver" means to dribble. The French do not like dry, stiff omelets but runny, squishy ones, so the drooling image refers to the texture of the omelet.

Salade de Pissenlit

You probably know that "pissenlit" is dandelion, but the literal translation cannot be denied. Besides, the Irish call it pissabed (because of its diuretic qualities). Actually, who wants to eat the stuff anyway? Can you imagine any dandelion leaves not having been pissed on by passing dogs?

Crottin

So, "crottin" can be horse or sheep turds; it also happens to be the name of a delightful little goat's cheese.

Le Puant de Lille

This cheese is noted for its strong odor of ammonia, but neither its smell nor its name seems to put consumers off.

Les Pets-de-nonne

Fritters to you and me but what a hilarious image. Actually I'm not so sure that "hilarious" is the right word . . . let's say disgusting, revolting, yukky . . .

Confiture de Gratte-cul

"Gratte-cul" is the haw, or fruit of the wild rose. It seems a shame to give it such an awful name.

Pisse-dru

A Beaujolais brand name.

BON APPETIT!

P.S. You could wash down the exquisite dessert with a sweet Sauterne wine whose particular composition comes from "la pourriture noble" (noble rot), the faint mold that appears on the skin of very ripe grapes when they are bursting with sugar. It is an integral part of the Sauterne winemaking process.

P.P.S. I can't resist adding (and this could be retaliatory ammunition for our Froggy friends) that my dear (English) husband has often asked me to prepare a dessert, the very idea of which I have been unable to stomach because of its repulsive name: spotted dick (ils sont fous, ces Anglais!). I still haven't brought myself to make it.

ANIMALS' NAMES TAKEN IN VAIN

Animal imagery plays a crucial role in the highly colorful expressions of colloquial French, often for negative associations: ugliness, stupidity, stubbornness, or nastiness. The star animals, those with the longest list of appearance in imagery, are inevitably (remembering those peasant origins of the French) domestic or farm animals, so they'll head our list.

avoir un mal de chien à faire quelque chose	to have a hell of a time in doing something
se donner un mal de chien pour faire quelque chose	to bend over backward to do something, to go out of one's way to do something
. . . de chien (e.g. une vie de chien, un temps de chien, un métier de chien)	lousy, rotten, crummy (e.g. a rotten existence, lousy weather, a crummy job)
avoir un caractère de chien	to have a nasty, aggressive disposition
malade comme un chien	as sick as a dog, very ill

AVOIR D'AUTRES CHATS À FOUETTER = TO HAVE OTHER FISH TO FRY

traiter quelqu'un comme un chien

to treat someone like dirt

mourir comme un chien

to die alone, without anyone to care for one

vivre comme chien et chat	fight like cats and dogs, to bicker constantly
être chien	to be stingy
avoir du chien	to have a certain chic
nom d'un chien!	darn!
faire la rubrique des chiens crevés	to be a journalist confined to reporting lowly, humdrum events (people's dead dogs, petty burglaries)
une vache, une peau de vache, une belle vache, une vraie vache	a hard, nasty, mean person
être vache avec quelqu'un	to be harsh, nasty to someone
c'est vache!	that's too bad, that's rotten
un coup de vache	a dirty, mean trick
manger de la vache enragée	to go through hard times (literally, to eat rabid cow)
une vache à lait	someone who is constantly milked by others, a patsy, a sucker
ça lui va comme un tablier à une vache	it looks awful, ridiculous on him/her (literally, it suits him/her as an apron would a cow)

pleuvoir comme vache qui pisse	to rain cats and dogs (literally, to rain like a cow pissing)
parler le français comme une vache espagnole	to speak pidgin French, to murder the French language
mort aux vaches!	down with the cops!
une vache à roulettes	a cop on wheels, a motorcycle cop
un veau	1. a lazy lump of a person 2. a nag (horse) 3. a tanklike car
pleurer comme un veau	to cry one's eyes out
souffler comme un boeuf	to breathe very heavily or with great difficulty
cochon(ne)	dirty (physically or mentally)
eh bien, mon cochon!	well, you devil!
faire un travail de cochon	to make a mess of something
faire un tour de cochon à quelqu'un	to play a dirty, nasty trick on someone
avoir un caractère de cochon	to be a difficult person

42

hé là, on n'a pas gardé les cochons ensemble!	hey, don't get so familiar! (literally, hey, we didn't keep pigs together)
c'est donner de la confiture à un cochon	it's throwing pearls before swine
être copains comme cochons	to be bosom buddies
des cochonneries ("Il ne raconte que des cochonneries.")	gross or revolting actions, dirty stories (All he tells are dirty stories)
de la cochonnerie ("C'est de la cochonnerie, ces tableaux!")	gargabe, trash (These paintings are a load of garbage!)
les moutons	white horses (the foam on the crests of waves)
les moutons de Panurge	people who follow others blindly, like sheep (Panurge is a Rabelaisian character)
le mouton à cinq pattes	the unattainable, the impossible
revenons à nos moutons	to get back to the subject
jouer à saute-mouton	to play leapfrog
la brebis galeuse	the "black sheep" (literally, the scabby sheep)

la crotte de bique ("Ta bagnole, c'est de la crotte de bique.")	junk, piece of crap (literally, goat droppings) (Your car's a lemon.)
une vieille bique	an old hag
mon biquet, ma biquette	baby, sweetheart, honey-lamb ("biquet" = kid goat)
une cage à lapins **une cabane à lapins**	a small, badly built dwelling; a rabbit hutch
ne pas valoir un pet de lapin	to be totally worthless (literally, not to be worth a rabbit fart)
c'est du lapinisme!	they have too many children! (reference, of course, to the reproductive capability of the rabbit)
poser un lapin à quelqu'un	to stand someone up
un chaud lapin	a hot-blooded male, a sex maniac
un nid-de-poule	a pothole
une poule mouillée	a scaredy-cat
avoir la chair de poule	to have goose pimples
une cage à poules	a cheaply, badly built dwelling, a chicken coop

44

se coucher aves les poules	to go to bed very early
avoir la bouche en cul-de-poule	to have pursed lips (literally, to have a mouth shaped like a hen's ass)
quand les poules auront des dents	never in a month of Sundays, when pigs fly (literally, when hens have teeth)
une poule	a tramp, a slut
mon poulet, ma poule	honey, sweetie, etc.
avoir des mollets de coq	to have wiry, skinny legs
sauter du coq à l'âne	to jump from one subject to another
une oie	a jerk
une oie blanche	an innocent, sweet young thing
les pattes d'oie	crow's feet
caca d'oie	greenish-yellow (literally, gooseshit)
ne pas casser quatre pattes à un canard	not to be worth writing home about (literally, not to break the four legs of a duck)
faire un froid de canard	to be freezing cold (weather and temperature only)

WHEN PIGS FLY

QUAND LES POULES AURONT
DES DENTS

un canard	1. a rag (newspaper)
	2. a sugar cube dunked in coffee or a liqueur and immediately eaten
	3. canard (false rumor, hoax)
un pigeon	a sucker, a dupe
se faire pigeonner	to be made a sucker, dupe of
couleur gorge-de-pigeon	a color with iridescent, changing glints as found on the feathers of a pigeon's throat
il n'y a pas un chat	there is not a soul around
il n'y a pas de quoi fouetter un chat	it's not worth making a big deal over (literally, it's not worth whipping a cat over it)
avoir d'autres chats à fouetter	to have more important things to do, to have other fish to fry
le chat, la chatte	the pussy (the female genitals)
appeler un chat un chat	to call a spade a spade
écrire comme un chat	to write illegibly and messily
avoir un chat dans la gorge	to have a frog in one's throat

AVOIR UN
CHAT DANS = TO HAVE
LA GORGE   A FROG IN
            ONE'S THROAT

du pipi de chat	an insipid or watered drink (literally, cat piss)
donner sa langue au chat	to give up (when faced with a riddle)
un âne	a stupid person, a jackass
faire/dire des âneries	to do/to say stupid things
le bonnet d'âne	the dunce's cap
monté comme un âne	to have a big cock, to be hung like a horse

48

du pipi d'âne	an insipid drink, horse piss
une tête de mule	a stubborn person of limited intelligence
un remède de cheval	a strong medicine that knocks one out, a kill-or-cure remedy
monter sur ses grands chevaux	to get on one's high horse
un grand cheval	a horse (describing a woman)
avoir une fièvre de cheval	to have a raging fever
être à cheval sur (le règlement, par exemple)	to be a stickler for (rules and regulations, for example)
entrer comme dans une écurie	to enter a room, a house, without acknowledging the presence of others
enculer les mouches	to split hairs, to nitpick (literally, to fuck a fly's ass)
tuer les mouches à quinze pas	to have bad breath; to have body odor (literally, to kill flies at fifteen paces)
les pattes de mouche	indecipherable, spidery, tiny scrawl
prendre la mouche	to fly off the handle, to get huffy

49

quelle mouche te pique?	what's eating you? what the hell's the matter with you?
avoir une araignée au plafond	to have bats in the belfry (literally, to have a spider on the ceiling)
une punaise de sacristie	a narrow-minded old woman who spends lots of time in church (literally, a sacristy bug)

une puce	a tiny person ("puce" = flea)
ma puce	term of affection for a small child
secouer les puces à quel-qu'un	to chew someone's ass out; rake someone over the coals
mettre la puce à l'oreille de quelqu'un	to awaken someone's suspicions, to put a bee in someone's bonnet
le pucier	the bed (i.e., the fleabag)
laid(e) comme un pou	very ugly, as ugly as sin (literally, as ugly as a louse)
minute, papillon!	hold it! hold your horses!
pas folle, la guêpe!	I'm/he's/she's nobody's fool! There are no flies on me/him/her ("guêpe" = wasp)

The wild is less well represented, its animals being less familiar than the domesticated ones. However, note:

bander comme un cerf	to have a huge erection (literally, to have an erection the size of a stag's)
ma biche	honey, sweetie ("biche" = doe)

avoir une faim de loup	to be ravenously hungry
avancer à pas de loup	to move stealthily
un drôle de zèbre	
un drôle d'oiseau	a weird fellow
un ours mal léché	a clumsy boor
vendre la peau de l'ours	to count your chickens before they're hatched
un chameau	an unpleasant, nasty person
un faisan	a crook, a shark
un vrai panier de crabes	a can of worms, a hornet's nest (figuratively)
un mollusque	an apathetic, dull weakling
une vieille guenon	an ugly old hag ("guenon" = female monkey)
on n'apprend pas à un singe comment faire la grimace	you can't teach an old dog new tricks (literally, you can't teach a monkey how to make faces)
malin comme un singe	very clever
payer en monnaie de singe	to reward with empty promises, with flowery language and nothing more (literally, to pay in monkey money)
laid(e) comme un singe	as ugly as sin

52

une girafe	a beanpole
une grenouille de béni-tier	a bigoted old woman who spends a lot of time in church (literally, a baptismal-font frog)
poisson d'avril!	April fool!

ANIMALSPEAK

No need to tell you that French dogs couldn't possibly go "bow-wow"—imagine, it would come out "bov-vov." If you wish to venture into the animal kingdom or sing "Old Mac-Donald" in French, you'd better learn some appropriate sounds. En France:

le chien fait **ouah ouah,**	le mouton fait **bêêê,**
le chat fait **miaou,**	la vache fait **meuh,**
le canard fait **coin-coin,**	l'âne **hi-han,**
la poule fait **cot-cot-cot-cot-cot,**	le hibou fait **hou hou,**
le coq fait **cocorico,**	la grenouille fait **crôâ crôâ**

Remember especially "cocorico," which is of national symbolic importance (see Chapter XI).

How about a few exercises to see how you are doing?

1. "Alors, maintenant, G. Leculgelé va nous présenter la météo." "Oui, eh bien, aujourd'hui, il fera un temps de

chien, il pleuvra comme vache qui pisse et demain, il fera un froid de canard."

2. Dis donc, vieille guenon, quelle mouche te pique?

3. Cet âne, je vais lui secouer les puces, il a encore fait un travail de cochon.

4. Je suis malade comme un chien, j'ai une fièvre de cheval et j'ai la chair de poule.

1. "And now, G. Frozenbutt will give us the weather forecast." "O.K., today it'll be rotten, it'll rain cats and dogs, and tomorrow it'll be freezing."

2. Hey, you old bag, what's eating you?

3. That jerk, I'm going to tell him off, he's made another mess.

4. I'm sick as a dog, I've got a raging fever and goose pimples.

VIII
ANATOMY OF A FROG:
A study of vital organs

No, we're not going to study *that* organ. While not denying its importance, other bits of the anatomy play an equally vital part in the behavior, psyche, pathology and, not least, language of the French.

THE LIVER

Most of you probably don't know the location or function of your liver, but the French are ever aware of its presence and concerned for its well-being. It is an essential part of their obsession with the digestive process—after all, if you have stuffed yourself with food, you have to be sure that it all goes down well. Have you ever suffered from a liver attack? The French do all the time: **"avoir une crise de foie"** is pure indigestion to you and me but, to the French, is more localized. To avoid the dreaded "crise de foie," much care is taken to aid and abet the digestive process. For example, a walk after a meal "pour la digestion" is deemed essential. Once, a French boy on a sailboat paced up and down after lunch, to the amazement of his British hosts; he explained that this was necessary "pour aider la digestion." More conveniently, post-prandial liqueurs are called **"digestifs"** and an Italian one, Fernet-Branca, finds great favor in France because of claims on its label that its mixture of herbs helps digestion—a clever alliance of medicine and pleasure.

Of course, carry the obsession with digestion to extremes, and one has to be concerned with the end product. See a doctor in France about any ailment and it is highly likely that he will ask whether you have been **"à la selle."** This is not a query about your riding ability (as "selle" = saddle, but here used to mean seat) but about your bowel movements. Note the following.

> **Avez-vous été à la selle aujourd'hui?** (Have you had a bowel movement today?)
>
> **Comment sont vos selles?** (How are your stools? Description of texture and color required, so be prepared.)

Patients may well leave the doctor's bearing a prescription not for our much-prized pills but for a box of suppositories. The French are not pill-poppers but suppository-shovers. Many a naive American or British patient in France has been found munching these waxy pellets in total ignorance of the destined orifice . . . now you know!

Here is some relevant vocabulary:

ça me donne une indigestion	I can't stand it, I'm fed up with it, I've had enough of it (said of any situation)
se faire de la bile	to worry oneself sick (literally, to produce bile, the secretion of the liver)

bilieux, bilieuse	irritable
le spleen	melancholy, the blues (though a different organ, the spleen ["la rate" in French] was also presumed to have an effect on one's moods—particularly the darker ones—and the use of this English word was popularized by Baudelaire in *Les Fleurs du mal*.)

THE NOSE

Listen to two famous Frenchmen:

Pascal: Le nez de Cléopâtre: s'il eût été plus long, toute la face de la terre aurait changé. (Cleopatra's nose: had it been longer, the entire face of the world would have changed.)

Edmond Rostand's character, Cyrano de Bergerac: . . . un grand nez est proprement l'indice/ D'un homme affable, bon, courtois, spirituel,/ Libéral, courageux. (. . . a great nose is truly the sign of a genial, good, courteous, witty, generous and brave man.)

Well, there we are. Don't underestimate the importance of the nose, especially when, like Frenchmen, you are endowed with a—what shall we say?—powerful, imposing one! Apart from its ability to change the course of world history, judge its place in the French view of things by the number of idioms it has . . . nosed its way into:

passer sous le nez de quelqu'un	to miss an opportunity ("**Ça m'est passé sous le nez.**" = I missed the opportunity, it slipped right through my fingers.)
ne pas mettre le nez dehors	not to go outside at all ("**Je n'ai pas mis le nez dehors de la journée.**" = I haven't been out all day.)
avoir le nez fin	to be shrewd
faire quelque chose les doigts dans le nez	to do something with great ease (literally, with one's fingers up one's nose)
mener quelqu'un par le bout du nez	to dominate someone, to do with someone as one pleases, lead him/her around by the nose
ne pas voir plus loin que le bout du nez	to lack foresight, not be able to see past the tip of one's nose
pendre au nez de quelqu'un	to be bound to happen to someone ("**Ça lui pend au nez.**" = He's got it coming to him.)
tirer les vers du nez de quelqu'un	to force someone to tell the truth (literally, to pull the worms from someone's nose)

58

se bouffer le nez	to have a violent quarrel (literally, to bite each other's noses off)
avoir un verre dans le nez	to be tipsy, to have had one too many
fourrer le nez dans les affaires des autres	to stick one's nose into other people's business
se trouver nez à nez avec quelqu'un	to bump into someone
faire quelque chose au nez de quelqu'un	to do something in front of another with impunity and/or cheek, do something right under someone's nose
rire au nez de quelqu'un	to laugh in someone's face
avoir la moutarde qui monte au nez	to get hot under the collar, to lose one's temper (literally, to have the mustard rise up one's nose)

THE TONGUE

Samuel Johnson said that "a Frenchman must always be talking, whether he knows anything of the matter or not." A Frenchman without a tongue is a contradiction in terms. Not only a tool of conversation, the tongue is, of course, used for tasting food and wine, for kissing ("French kissing"), and for having a good gossip (a favorite French pastime). A few idioms:

une mauvaise langue	a gossip
tirer la langue	to be dying of thirst (therefore, one's tongue is hanging out); by extension, to be in great need (do not confuse with **"tirer la langue à quelqu'un"** = to stick one's tongue out at someone)
avoir la langue bien pendue	to be very talkative, to have the gift of the gab
se mordre la langue	1. to hold oneself back from saying something, to bite one's tongue 2. to regret having said something
ne pas avoir sa langue dans sa poche	never to be at a loss for words (**"ce mec n'a pas sa langue dans sa poche."** = that guy's always got something to say.)
donner sa langue au chat	to give up (in games, riddles, etc.)

"LE DERRIÈRE"

If you remember from *MERDE!* the importance of the backside ("le cul" = ass) and of the scatological in everyday vocabulary (knowledge of which is fundamental to the understanding of many a French joke), you will not be surprised to find a number of expressions emanating from that part of the French anatomy:

avoir du cul	to be lucky
l'avoir dans le cul	to be unlucky
avoir quelqu'un dans le cul	to despise someone
en avoir plein le cul	to be fed up with someone or something
en rester sur le cul	to be utterly amazed by something
tirer au cul	to be lazy, to get away with doing as little as possible (gives the noun "**un tire-au-cul**")
avoir du poil au cul	to be brave, gutsy (literally, to have hair on one's ass)
péter plus haut que son cul	to think too highly of oneself (literally, to fart higher than one's ass)
un lèche-cul	an ass kisser
un cul béni	a devout Catholic
un cul terreux	a peasant
avoir chaud aux fesses **serrer les fesses**	to be scared ("les fesses" = butt)

attraper quelqu'un par la peau des fesses	to catch someone by the scruff of the neck

OTHER ORGANS: A LINGUISTIC POTPOURRI

Other bits and pieces of the body figure prominently and commonly in idioms, so away we go:

tomber sur un os	to hit a snag
il y a un os	there's a hitch
en avoir par-dessus la tête	to be fed up with someone or something
se casser la tête (à faire quelque chose)	to rack one's brains (doing something)
avoir une tête à claques	to have an unpleasant, stupid, stubborn mien, such that one feels the urge to slap it ("claques" = slaps)
n'en faire qu'à sa tête	to do only as one pleases, to go one's merry way
faire la tête, faire la gueule	to sulk
une tête/une gueule d'enterrement	a long, sad face (literally, a funereal mien)
avoir la tête enflée	to have a swollen, fat head; to be pleased with oneself

avoir une sale tête	to have a nasty, unpleasant look about one
casser la tête (à quelqu'un)	to get on someone's nerves
tenir à un cheveu	to hang by a thread ("**Il n'en tenait qu'à un cheveu.**" = It was touch and go.)
avoir un cheveu sur la langue	to lisp
ça te défrise?	any objection? (literally, does it take the curl out of your hair?)
une grande gueule	a loudmouth
ne pas desserrer les dents	to clam up, to refuse to talk
se casser les dents	to fail
avoir une dent contre quelqu'un	to bear a grudge against someone
avoir la dent dure	to be hard and critical
avoir la dent	to be hungry
avoir les dents longues	to be very hungry
n'avoir rien à se mettre sous la dent	to have nothing to eat (in the house)
être sur les dents	to be overworked

casser les oreilles à quel-qu'un	to deafen someone ("**Tu me casses les oreilles avec ta musique.**" = Your music is deafening me.)
ce n'est pas tombé dans l'oreille d'un sourd	it didn't fall on deaf ears
mettre la puce à l'oreille de quelqu'un	to raise someone's suspicions, to put a bee in someone's bonnet
coûter les yeux de la tête	to cost an arm and a leg
s'en battre l'oeil	not to give a damn about something
ne pas avoir froid aux yeux	to be gutsy
tourner de l'oeil	1. to faint 2. to go bad ("**Ta crème tourne de l'oeil.**" = Your cream is going sour. "**Ta plante tourne de l'oeil.**" = Your plant is looking a bit sad.)
avoir quelqu'un à l'oeil	to keep a close watch on someone
ne pas avoir les yeux dans sa poche	to see and notice everything, to have one's wits about one
faire les gros yeux	to scold

64

COÛTER LES YEUX DE LA TÊTE

$ 10,100

TO COST AN ARM AND A LEG

ça saute aux yeux, ça crève les yeux	it's really obvious
se mettre le doigt dans l'oeil (jusqu'au coude)	to put one's foot in something; to be grossly clumsy or mistaken (literally, to put one's finger in one's eye—up to the elbow).
à l'oeil	free, gratis
taper dans l'oeil de quelqu'un	to click with someone, to hit it off
faire la petite bouche	to turn up one's nose
une fine bouche, une fine gueule	a gourmet
avoir un chat dans la gorge	to have a frog in one's throat
ça m'est/lui est resté dans la gorge	I/he/she found it hard to take, to swallow
jusqu'au cou	completely, seriously ("être dans la merde jusqu'au cou" = to be in deep trouble, "être endetté jusqu'au cou" = to be in debt up to one's neck)
avoir le bras long	to have influence, to have the right contacts

avoir quelqu'un/quelque chose sur les bras	to be saddled with someone/something
gros(sc) comme le bras	unsubtle (**"une flatterie grosse comme le bras"** = unsubtle, obvious flattery)
les bras m'en tombent!	I'm amazed, I can't believe it! (literally, it makes my arms fall off!)
être dans les bras de Morphée	to be asleep
j'en mettrais ma main au feu	I am absolutely certain of it, I'd stake my life on it (literally, I'd put my hand in the fire)
ne pas y aller de main morte	not to do something halfway (**"Il n'y va pas de main morte quand il se sert un verre."** = He sure pours himself a stiff drink.)
prendre quelque chose/quelqu'un en main	to take charge of something/someone
mettre la main à la pâte	to roll up one's sleeves (literally, to put one's hand to the dough)
faire des pieds et des mains pour faire quelque chose	to move heaven and earth to do something

avoir quelque chose sous la main	to have something within arm's reach, at hand
se mordre les doigts	to be impatient, to be annoyed
s'en mordre les doigts	to regret something, to kick oneself for something (an action, a nasty word)
être comme les deux doigts de la main	to be very close (people)
mon petit doigt me l'a dit	a little bird told me
ne pas remuer le petit doigt	not to lift a finger
être à un doigt/deux doigts de la mort	to be at death's door
pouce!	time! (to call a halt to a game, to pause)
se tourner les pouces	to twiddle one's thumbs
un coup de pouce	a little push, i.e. help ("il lui faudra un petit coup de pouce pour avoir une promotion" = He'll need someone to put in a good word for him if he's to get a promotion.)
avoir les ongles en deuil	to have dirty fingernails ("le deuil" = mourning)

68

(être quelque chose) **jus-qu'au bout des ongles**	(to be something) totally, to one's fingertips ("**Il est socialo jusqu'au bout des ongles.**" = He's an out-and-out socialist.)
la Veuve Poignet	masturbation ("**aller voir la Veuve Poignet**" = to masturbate; "la veuve" = the widow, "le poignet" = the wrist)
lever le coude	to be a heavy drinker ("le coude" = the elbow)
se serrer les coudes	to stick together and help one another
jouer des coudes	to elbow one's way
épauler	to give support
donner un coup d'épaule à quelqu'un	to help someone to succeed, to lend someone a helping hand
en avoir plein le dos	to be fed up with something/someone
se mettre quelqu'un à dos	to make an enemy out of someone
avoir bon dos	to be unfairly blamed ("**il a bon dos le train**" = the train makes a good excuse, doesn't it?)

69

il a une poitrine de vélo	he's a 98-pound weakling
joli comme un coeur	lovely, sweet, cute
prendre/avoir quelque chose à coeur	to take a passionate interest in something
tenir à coeur de quelqu'un	to hold great interest for someone (**"Ce projet lui tient à coeur."** = He really has his heart set on this project).
loin des yeux, loin du coeur	out of sight, out of mind (notice that emotions feature in the French expression whereas thoughts do in the English)
avoir des haut-le-coeur	to be on the verge of throwing up
avoir quelque chose dans le ventre	to have guts, courage, balls
se mettre à plat ventre devant quelqu'un	to be obsequious toward someone, to crawl, to toady
le bas-ventre	euphemism for the genital area (as in "nether regions")
autant pisser dans un violon	it's a waste of time, there's no point, it's like banging your head against a brick wall

ça lui a pris comme une envie de pisser	he did it out of the blue (literally, he did it as suddenly as a need to piss)
faire des ronds de jambe à quelqu'un	to bow and scrape in front of someone
tenir la jambe à quel-qu'un	to buttonhole someone
cela me (te/lui/nous/ vous/leur) fait une belle jambe	a fat lot of good it does me (you/her, him/us/you/ them)
se croire sorti(e) de la cuisse de Jupiter	to think one is God's gift to mankind
être sur les genoux	to be exhausted, to be on one's knees
avoir les chevilles enflées	to be pleased with oneself (literally, to have swollen ankles)
ne pas lui arriver aux chevilles	to be inferior to him/her
faire du genou/du pied	to play kneesies, footsies
prendre son pied	to have an orgasm
bête comme ses pieds	really stupid
(faire quelque chose) comme un pied	(to do something) really badly, clumsily
ça te/vous fera les pieds!	that'll teach you!

se lever du pied gauche	to get out of bed on the wrong side, to start the day off badly
de pied ferme	with determination
partir au pied levé	to leave without adequate preparation (" **partir en guerre au pied levé**" = to go off to war totally unprepared)
mettre les pieds dans le plat	to stick one's foot in it
ne pas savoir sur quel pied danser	1. not to know how to react or what to expect (" **Avec la belle-doche, on ne sait jamais sur quel pied danser.**" = You never know what to expect with a mother-in-law.)
	2. to be undecided, to be of two minds
je t'emmerde à pied, à cheval et en voiture	you can go to hell for all I care ("emmerder quel-qu'un" = to give someone a pain in the ass—remember *MERDE!* The list of forms of transport simply shows the totality of the feeling.)
casser les pieds à quel-qu'un	to give someone a pain in the neck

72

FROG PATHOLOGY

MEDICINE

Examine a Frenchman's medicine chest and you will find amazing numbers of medicines, many of which can be bought over the counter. Great faith is placed in the effect of medicine, and the subject animates many a conversation. The French have a high rate of "placebo effect": experiments have shown that 40 percent of French ulcer sufferers were cured by placebos.

HYGIENE

It's *official*: stink-factor, what many foreigners have complained of, the . . . er . . . lack of hygiene of the French, has been confirmed by research! Yes, scientific studies conducted by the French themselves have revealed that the average Frog uses only 2.25 bars of soap a year. If you hear "savon" in a conversation it most likely has nothing to do with soap but with an unpleasant situation: **"passer un savon à quelqu'un"** = to give someone a real telling off, a real piece of one's mind. Now *that* "savon" gets used frequently, you can be sure!

Worse than the news about soap is the revelation that toothbrushes are purchased at the rate of one for every three persons a year! Fifty per cent of them go to bed without brushing their teeth! A *French* journalist wrote recently that many Frenchmen smell like kangaroos kept in cages. French kings' stink is well chronicled: One of the recordholders was Henri IV, whose odor nearly made his fiancée, Marie de' Medici, faint on their first meeting. She had covered her own body heavily with fragrances from her native Italy but they proved an insufficient barrage.

Are the French ashamed of their smell? Not really. Why, many think it is sexy. Napoleon wrote to Josephine from Egypt, where he had been campaigning, "Ne te lave pas, j'arrive." (Don't wash, I'm coming.) Consider, if you will,

73

how many weeks it would have taken for him to arrive back in France . . . if smell was what turned him on, he was in for a good time!

DEATH

The Frenchman's natural irreverence as well as his penchant for drama provide the impetus for a rich vocabulary to convey the notion of death. A news report will not say simply that so-and-so died or passed away but that he disappeared ("a disparu") or left us ("nous a quittés"), as though the fellow had done it on purpose. Announcement of death often takes the form: "Tartempion n'est plus" (so-and-so is no more). Here, then, to express the final voyage:

> **Sartre n'est plus** (present tense only, to announce the event as it happens), **nous a été enlevé, est mort, est décédé, a disparu, nous a quittés, a été rappelé devant Dieu** (well, not applicable to M. Sartre), **a trépassé, s'est éteint, a été emporté** (accompanied by the name of the illness as in "a été emporté par le cancer").

Or, irreverently:

> **Sartre bouffe les pissenlits par la racine** (notice that in English one says *"pushing* up daisies," whereas the French talk of eating), **a cassé sa pipe, a crevé, a cla-mecé, a claqué, y est resté, a passé l'arme à gauche, a avalé son bulletin de naissance** (swallowed his birth certificate).

So long, buddy!

IX
APPEE BEURZDÉ TOOH YOOH:
Franglais as she is spoke

The good news (for you English-speakers) is that Franglais is expanding daily. If the Frogs go on like this, you won't have to bust your guts trying to learn their language.

The bad news is that you have to learn their funny pronunciation (viz. the chapter heading—Frogpronunciation for "Happy Birthday to You," which is sung up and down the land) as well as the arbitrary gender they give the purloined words. The following is a basic list of real Franglais.

l'after-shave (m.)

le badge

le barbecue

les baskets (= sneakers)

le beefsteack (*sic*), le bifteck

le best-seller

le black-out

le blue-jean

les blues

le bluff

le box-office

le break (= a station wagon)

le bridge (= dental bridge/ card game)

le bulldozer

le bungalow

le caddy (= the supermarket cart)

le cake (= fruitcake)

la call-girl

le car-ferry

le club

le cocktail

la cover-girl

le cover-story

un crack (= a wizard, an ace)

le dancing

le design

le détective

le discount

le doping

l'escalator (m.)

l'establishment (m.)

le fair-play

les fans

le fast-food

le feedback

le flash

le fuel (heating oil)

le gadget

le gangster

le garden-center

le gay

le gentleman

le hall

le handicap

le hit-parade

le hold-up

le hooligan

l'interview (f.)

le jerry-can

le jogging

le joker (in cards)

le kidnapping

le kit

le knock-out

le label

le leader

le lifting (the facelift)

le living (= the living room)

le look

le magazine

le manager

le marketing

les mass-media (m.)

le music-hall

le must

le name-dropping

LE DANCING

LE SEX-APPEAL

LE LOOK

LE MAGAZINE

LE SWEATSHIRT

JAZZ

LE TOP DU HIT-PARADE

LE LABEL

LA PIN-UP

LE BLUE-JEAN

LES BASKETS

le one-man-show	**le puzzle**
l'outsider (m.) (in a race)	**le racket** (the illegal one)
le pacemaker	**se relaxer**
le parking	**le scoop** (journalistic)
le patchwork	**la script-girl**
le pickpocket	**select(e)** (adj.)
la pin-up	**le self-made-man**
le planning	**le self-service**
le playback	**le sex-appeal**
le play-boy	**sexy**
le pressing (= the dry cleaners)	**le short** (= shorts)

78

le show business

le sketch (in entertainment)

le slogan

le snack (= snack bar)

snob

le software

le sponsoring

le spot publicitaire (= the ad)

squattériscr, lc squat

le standing (= status)

la starlet, la star

le stock

le stop (= thumbing a lift, hitchhiking)

stopper (to stop)

le stress

le studio (= one-room apartment)

le supporter

le sweatshirt

le talkie-walkie (*sic*)

le time-sharing

le traveler's cheque

le week-end

These sentences should be no problem:

1. Le cover-story du magazine décrit le best-seller qui va faire partie du name-dropping littéraire aux dîners de Paris.

2. Le look de la saison est un véritable patchwork de styles.

3. Le sketch montrait des pickpockets dans un squat.

P.S. Add to the list most sporting terms, too numerous to be mentioned here (for example, le sprint, le tennis, le crawl, le recordman, le score, le match, and so on).

X
ALLONS ENFANTS:
Kids and kiddie talk

THE AU PAIR'S GUIDE TO KIDDIE TALK

"Mémé, le toutou, il m'a fait bobo." "Tonton m'a fait panpan parce que j'ai fait pipi dans mon dodo." Got it? If you're going to take care of the little brats, you'd better learn to communicate with them, so the following is required knowledge.

mémé	granny
pépé	grampa
tonton	uncle
tata	aunt
au dodo!	off to bed!
faire dodo	to sleep
le lolo	milk

le nounours	the teddy bear
avoir bobo	to have something that hurts (**"T'as bobo à la papatte?"** = Does your little leg/hand hurt?)
un bobo	a sore
la menotte	the hand
la papatte	the leg/the hand
les quenottes (f.)	the teeth
le toto	the head louse
le loulou	snot
le zizi	the genitals (male or female)
pipi (m.)	wee-wee, number one
caca (m.) la grosse commission	poopie, number two
un prout	a fart
faire panpan	to smack
le toutou	the doggy
le joujou	the toy
faire joujou	to play
faire sisite	to sit down

To talk to small children in the idiotic way many adults do, simply repeat part or all of one-syllable words: "fifille," "chienchien," "papatte" . . . . Note that use of the above vocabulary is not confined to the kiddie community, as you may recall from previous chapters, where mention is made of "caca d'oie" and "métro-boulot-dodo." Many of these words also appear in satirical contexts, so to understand adult jokes, apply yourself to learning kiddie vocabulary.

"LE FRANÇAIS MÉPRISE LA JEUNESSE"

Jean Cocteau
Picasso
Editions Stock

Do Frogs like children? I am not terribly convinced they do. Before I get pelted with tomatoes by indignant Frogesses, could I simply ask you to draw your own conclusion from the large number of abusive terms used to describe children? Our "brats" is nothing compared with the variety of French names that have the same meaning but are too often used instead of "kids." For a start, even the normal words for "kids" (**"les gosses," "les mômes," "les gamins"**) are often preceded by "sales" (dirty; used here for lousy, rotten), which does not denote great tenderness. The following all mean "brats," have a note of unpleasant irony, can equally be preceded by "sales," and are quite commonly used:

les lardons (m.)

les mioches (m., f.)

les marmots (m.)

les mouflets, mouflettes

les rejetons (m.)

les moutards (m.)

les morveux (m., f.) (literally, the snot-nosed)

les chiards (m.) (literally, the crappers)

la marmaille (a group of noisy children)

82

Their native impatience prevents the French from putting themselves at children's level. They are easily irritated and can be very agile at distributing **"les claques," "les gifles"** (slaps in the face). On the reverse side of the coin, the media often descend to maudlin, glutinous sentimentality, talking of "nos chérubins" or "nos petites têtes blondes" (they cannot be serious!). A final note, and conclude from it what you will: France has the second-worst record (after Hungary) for accidents in the home involving children.

XI
THE COCORICO
SYNDROME:
Roosters rule ok

*"Qu'est-ce que la France, je vous le demande? Un coq
sur un fumier. Otez le fumier, le coq meurt."* (What is
France, I ask you? A rooster on a dung heap. Take
away the dung, and the rooster dies.)

Jean Cocteau
La Difficulté d'être
Editions du Rocher

*". . . forgive me, God,
That I do brag thus! This your air of France
Hath blown that vice in me."*

Shakespeare
Henry V

It seems a strange idea, though perhaps an appropriate
one, to have a rooster—that vain, strutting, loudmouthed,
ridiculous creature—as a national symbol. Napoleon's eagle
was certainly a more dignified idea, though he got his feathers
plucked just as surely as the neighborhood barnyard rooster.

The Latin word *gallus* provides the symbol, "gallus" being at the same time "the Gaul" and "the rooster." No fools those Romans, they had already remarked upon the Gauls' loquacity as well as their querulous, aggressive nature. Tacitus reckoned that if the Gauls had stopped quarreling among themselves they would have been nearly invincible.

What other manifestations are there of what one could call the "cocorico syndrome"? Before I am accused of slander, allow me to point out that every year books are published in France analyzing and usually criticizing the French character and how it affects the individual's and the country's life; the French, given to self-analysis (**"le nombrilisme"** = navel contemplation), are quite aware of their defects and are sometimes even proud of them.

At the national level, the cocorico syndrome is revealed in the need to win acclaim, to have France's "destiny" and importance to the world recognized. It has made some Frenchmen say the most extraordinary things across the ages, such as:

> "La gloire de la France est un des plus nobles ornements du monde." (France's glory is one of the world's most noble adornments.)
>
> Montaigne

Mr. Supercocorico himself, General de Gaulle, was forever proclaiming France synonymous with grandeur and reckoned that she existed to "illuminate" the universe.

The press still talks of **"l'honneur de la France"** and sees failures or setbacks as humiliations. It is interesting to see how the "cocorico syndrome" has affected the French reading of history. Of course, each country has a selective memory for historical dates. Here are a few that are firmly imprinted on the national psyche, not all of them victorious moments either, though François Ier had a comforting word about that. Faced with defeat at Pavia, he exclaimed: "Tout est perdu fors l'honneur" (All is lost save honor) . . . to each his own priorities.

AD 52   Alésia: Vercingétorix, valiant leader of the Gauls, is beaten by the "sales" (i.e., rotten) Romans, who drag him back to Rome and execute him.

732   (Cocorico!) Charles Martel kicks out the "sales" Saracens at Poitiers.

1214   (Cocorico!) Philippe Auguste socks it to the "sales" league of English, Flemish and Germans at Bouvines.

1431   The "sales" English burn our girl, Jeanne d'Arc.

1515   (Cocorico!) François Ier socks it to the Swiss at Marignano.

1789   (Cocorico!) The French infuse the world with the spirit of liberty, equality, and fraternity.

1792   (Cocorico!) The people's army routs the foreign enemy at Valmy.

1870   Defeat at Sedan at the hands of the "sales Boches."

1898   The "sales" English humiliate us at Fashoda (Sudan).

1940   The "sales" Brits treacherously sink our fleet at Mers-el-Kebir.

At the individual level, we get "le Français frondeur" (anti-authority, ever critical), the opinionated, querulous, restless, contradictory undisciplined worshiper of speech who easily substitutes words for action. Shakespeare and Walpole knew a thing or two about "the confident and over-lusty French" (Shakespeare) and "their insolent and unfounded airs of superiority" (Walpole). Ah, now, speaking of lust, what of that worldwide, self-proclaimed reputation in this field?

The rooster makes a lot of noise and services many hens, but does he satisfy them? He obviously thinks so:

87

"Le Français est un mâle supérieur . . . comme amant il crée partout." (The Frenchman is a superior male . . . as a lover, he is ever creative.)

Jules Michelet
(nationalist historian 1798–1874)

"Le français . . . c'est la langue même des dieux, la seule dans laquelle un homme puisse laisser entendre à une femme qu'il l'aime." (French . . . is the very language of the gods, the only one in which a man can make a woman understand that he loves her.)

Maurice Bedel
(writer 1884–1954)

The Frenchman's ability in what he considers a sport and an art form resides, as with his intellectual pursuits, more in form than in content. Murmuring sweet poetic nothings that would make anyone swoon with rapture is one of his prize talents . . . yet what good is it to be told that one is a fellow's eternal love when he omits to add "eternal love number 598"? To the Frenchman, adultery is an accepted fact of life, and the absence of extramarital pursuits might cast doubts on one's virility.

Despite the leering, the coveting of the neighbor's wife and the view of sex as proof of sporting prowess and artistic creativity, there are numerous maudlin articles in the press about celebrities' fairytale loves. Nobody actually believes them but everyone still reads the stuff.

The "cocorico syndrome" in its egocentric aspect produces the legendary rudeness and the notorious shoving ahead of one's place in line. A recent European poll is revealing: in a list of seventeen qualities to be ranked in order of importance, the French put manners in only tenth place.

Who says the French don't play much sport? It just depends on one's definition of sport. The expression **"c'est tout un sport"** has nothing to do with athletic pursuits; it refers to the great effort necessary to accomplish something, as in "C'est

tout un sport de lui plaire" (It's very difficult to please him/
her).

Recognized national sports are **"la resquille"** (getting
something to which one has no right, getting away without
paying for something; for example, fare evasion), **"la com-
bine"** (scheming, beating the system, working around regula-
tions for one's own benefit), and **"rouler le fisc"** (cheating on
one's taxes). It follows from acceptance of these activities that
the French are ever **"méfiants"** (distrustful, suspicious) and
that one of their reflexes is to search for what might be con-
cealed underneath an action or a proposal. The European
values study showed that 71 percent of the French believe that
people cannot be trusted. The rules of the aforementioned
sports allow for **"la dénonciation"** (denunciation), a favorite
French activity, along with its offshoot, calumny. Both make
much use of the anonymous letter and reached their heyday
under the German occupation in World War II.

The study also confirmed the importance of **"l'épargne"**
(thrift). Indeed, the **"image d'Épinal"** (= stereotype; from
the popular prints depicting typical scenes from French life,
which came from Épinal from the eighteenth century onward)
of the French includes the love of a good bargain (**"la bonne
affaire"**) and an attachment to gold. There is a fortune of
4,500 tons of gold in private hands in France, as much as for
the rest of Europe put together.

Speaking of gold, what are the gold-medal achievements of
our fine-feathered friends, the **"cocoricorecords"** (a term
coined by the magazine *Nouvel Observateur*)?

1. The second-highest alcohol intake in the world.

2. The highest rate of cirrhosis of all industrialized countries
   (our friend the liver strikes again).

3. The second-highest number of car accidents per head of
   population, a statistic not unrelated to the first record but
   by no means totally explained by it. The "cocorico syndrome" as it emerges in French driving habits deserves a
   special note.

A COCORICO NOTE: FROGS ON WHEELS

Be prepared: the French are selfish, macho drivers who tail-gate ("**coller aux fesses**"). They flash their headlights and honk their horns in an ever-present urge to overtake and speed away to the next traffic light. The women are as aggressive as the men, and the owners of small cars get orgasmic thrills out of overtaking more powerful Mercedes, BMWs, and the like. It might be useful to know some relevant vocabulary, and don't forget to perfect your "bras d'honneur" (see Chapter III). You will need it to express your indignation at nasty French driving. But since it requires the use of both hands, it might be better to teach it to your passengers so that, unlike the Frogs, you can keep your hands on the wheel.

un chauffard	a reckless, bad driver
faire une queue de poisson	to overtake and cut in close in front of the car you are overtaking (literally, to do a fishtail)
appuyer sur le champignon	to step on it, to put one's foot down on the accelerator (literally, to press down on the mushroom, from the shape of certain old-fashioned pedals)
conduire à la vitesse grand V	to drive at great speed, to go like a bat out of hell
brûler/griller le feu rouge	to go through a red light, to jump the lights

rentrer dans le décor   to drive off the road into a ditch, a tree, etc. (the consequence of the previous activities; "le décor" = the scenery)

se payer un arbre, un piéton   to drive right into a tree, to run over a pedestrian

cette bagnole bouffe de l'essence	this car is a gas-guzzler
c'est un vrai tape-cul	it's a bone-shaker (literally, it's a real ass-thumper)
un tacot **un teuf-teuf**	an old, slow-moving car
une bagnole poussive	a slow car
une contredanse **un PV** (un procès-verbal)	a ticket

It is worth knowing that French license plates ("**plaques minéralogiques**") give a clue to the driver's place of residence: the last two numbers correspond to his "département" or, in the case of Paris, to the city itself or its suburbs. The magic number is 75 ("ville de Paris") whose proud bearers can look in condescension on the Parisian suburbanites with their 78 (Yvelines), 91 (Essonne), 92 (Hauts-de-Seine), 93 (Seine-Saint-Denis), 94 (Val-de-Marne) and 95 (Val-d'Oise). All of these can in turn look down with pity or contempt on any other number. On the other hand, driving around the provinces with Parisian number plates can attract "**des remarques désobligeantes**" (unpleasant remarks) about "**ces sales Parigots**" (those Parisian bastards), given that their driving is even more selfish and aggressive than the national average.

Finally, if you want to be like the French, you may scoff at cars sporting the B sticker (Belgium) or the CH (Switzerland, or "cantons helvétiques") as the French love railing at these peoples' slow, clumsy driving.

XII
GEOGRAPHY À
LA FRANÇAISE:
A linguistic study

PROFESSOR FRANCHOUILLARD'S*
GEOGRAPHY LESSON

Let's listen in to Professor Franchouillard's very own, very typical geography lesson on foreign countries.

Prof. Franchouillard: I shall tell you a joke. There once was a Belgian . . . hee, hee, ha, ha . . . (*He breaks into uncontrollable fits of laughter.*)

We, the audience: Are you all right?

Prof. Franchouillard: Yes, yes, ah mon dieu . . . There was once a Swiss . . (*More uncontrollable laughter.*)

Audience: Please, what can we do for you?

Prof. Franchouillard (regaining his composure):   Listen, the English among you would say "There's this Irishman," the Americans would say "There's this Pole." Eh bien, nous, on

* Franchouillard = colloquial French for Frenchman, i.e., Frenchy.

dit "Y'a un Belge," "Y'a un Suisse," because the Belgians and
the Swiss are so stupid, so thick, so slow! They have such
funny accents! They say such funny things as "septante" (sev-
enty) and "nonante" (ninety).

A student: Excuse me, sir, isn't it easier and more logical to
say "septante" and "nonante" than "soixante-dix" and "quatre-
vingt-dix"?

Prof. Franchouillard: Ta gueule ou je te fous mon pied au
cul (shut up or you'll get a kick in the ass). Now, speaking as
we were of those "sales Anglais," we and our language know
how to deal with them! No need to remind you of **"filer à
l'anglaise"** (to take French leave) and **"la capote anglaise"**
(French letter). But do you know what **"avoir ses anglais"** or
"les Anglais débarquent" (literally, the English have
landed) mean? Ha, ha, ha, it means a woman's period has
started!!! See in the image the suddenness of the flow of red-
coats and the notion of invasion . . . brilliant, n'est-ce pas?
As for **"le vice anglais,"** that's homosexuality (or, sometimes,
flagellation), and **"anglaiser"** means to sodomize, to bugger
. . . after all, we French know that the English are all fags.
And such hypocrites! In their honor, we have the expression
"le coup de Trafalgar," which really means an unexpected
catastrophe but is popularly used to mean an underhand trick,
because the English are always playing dirty with their double-
dealing, perfidious underhandedness. Anyway, we almost won
Trafalgar and Waterloo, and we got that asshole Nelson!

A student: Have you any more world views to impart to us?

Prof. Franchouillard: If you have learned your lessons in our
first textbook, *MERDE!*, you will know all about **"les
Boches, les Amerloqs, les Ritals, les Rastaquouères, les
Ruskis, les Bougnoules, les Bicots,"** and so on. As for our
views on others, apart from the Belgians, the Swiss, and the
English we're not all that bothered, except that, nowadays, we
slavishly idolize everything American, all the while maintain-
ing our belief in our own intellectual superiority. But we do
have a few expressions that will come in handy:

une querelle d'Allemand	a quarrel started for no good or obvious reason (a throwback to the continuous and petty quarrels of the German princelings of old)
soûl comme un Polonais	blind drunk
avoir l'oeil américain	to have a sharp eye
c'est pas le Pérou	it's not a fortune, it's not a great deal of money, one won't get rich on that
une tête de Turc	a scapegoat, a whipping boy
fort comme un Turc	strong as a horse
le téléphone arabe	to spread a rumor by word of mouth
c'est de l'hébreu **c'est du chinois**	it's all Greek to me
les chinoiseries (f.)	1. unnecessary, hairsplitting complications 2. red tape
un casse-tête chinois	a real puzzle, a real headache
un supplice chinois	a cruel and refined torture, Chinese water-torture
boire en Suisse	to drink alone, in secret

point d'argent, point de Suisse	if there's no money to be had, there'll be no Swiss around
va te/allez vous faire voir chez les Grecs!	go get fucked! (cf. the ancient Greeks' homosexual leanings)

In contrast to the above, and quite rightly so, you should know that the word "français" appears in favorable expressions (Cocorico!):

en bon français	to put it simply
vous ne comprenez pas le français, non?	can't you understand when one speaks to you? (i.e., why are you so thick?)
impossible n'est pas français	the word "impossible" is not in the French language
une histoire gauloise	a dirty story, a risqué story

NOTES ON THE NATIVES

Everyone knows that there are two basic types of French people: the Parisians and all the rest, "les provinciaux," those poor second-class citizens given to staring incessantly and enviously at the bright center of all political, economic, cultural, financial, and educational life, all the while denouncing "le parisianisme" (the assumption that only Paris is deserving of one's attention). The stereotypical characteristics of the French are exaggerated in the Parisian, who adds to them a heavy dose of arrogance.

Two main forms of snobbery can be found in Paris (overlapping is possible), so let's have a look.

GALLUS LUTETIAE SNOBINARDUS
(Lutetia = Latin for Paris)

This is the moneyed and/or aristocratic branch.

HABITAT:
"Les beaux quartiers," which are basically the XVIe arrondissement, with some streets of the neighboring VIIIe, and some streets of the old VIe (Latin Quarter).

MIGRATORY PATTERN:
to the "château" or other "résidence secondaire."

DESIGNATION IN ORDER OF PREFERENCE:
1. A title, however bogus or "du côté gauche" (from the wrong side of the blanket, the term for titles conferred on the numerous illegitimate offspring of kings, princes, cardinals, and so on).

2. "La particule," the prized "de." These two letters, which originally meant nothing more than that their bearer came from a certain village, have acquired such an aura of grandeur that people search desperately for some ancestor who had such a "de," so that it can be tagged on to their own names. Or, if worse comes to worst, one can always insert it with impunity or change the spelling of one's name, just as Napoleon III's illegitimate half-brother, who was born Demorny, changed the spelling of his name to "de Morny" and called himself "duc"—so much more dignified.

3. A double-barreled name—and all the better if the barrels contain a "de," as in Madame de la Connerie de Merde.

4. Choice of first names. Exotic or medieval names set one aside from **"la populace," "le menu fretin," "le populo," "les gens communs,"** you know, ordinary people.

97

To demonstrate the above, let us examine the births, engagements, and marriages page of the *Figaro*, particularly on a Saturday. Take Saturday, 26 January 1985: on that day, "Le Carnet du Jour" listed twenty-three engagements, fourteen of which contained one or all of the previously mentioned assets. Example:

> Le vicomte Hugues de Monts de Savasse et la vicomtesse, née Chantal de Fournas de la Brosse, M. Yves du Mesnildot et Mme., née Marie de La Bourdonnaye, sont heureux d'annoncer les fiançailles de leurs enfants. . . .

As for the births section, exotic or medieval names given to the newborn were Typhanie, Apollonia, Colombe, Fleur, Solène, Amaury, Aliénor, Héloïse.

SPEECH:
The height of rarefied elegance, becoming thankfully very rare indeed, is attained by those parents who make their children address them by the formal pronoun "vous." It could result in "Maman, vous m'emmerdez!"

The tone of our "snobinardus" friend is not the braying of the English aristocracy but a more refined, slow, measured, assured tone of voice, delivery accompanied by the slight hooding of the eyes and an upward tilt of the nose. Useful long words to express one's amazement at another's vulgarity or stupidity:

d'une vulgarité, d'une bêtise	**inénarrable**	**sidérante**
	faramineuse	**suffoquante**
	monumentale	**époustou-** **flante**
	prodigieuse	**hallucinante**
	phénoménale	**grotesque**
	ineffable	**aberrante**
	inouïe	**épouvantable**

All give the notion of "extraordinary" and/or "breathtaking."

98

GALLUS LUTETIAE INTELLO-SNOBINARDUS

This creature can belong to the previous crowd, but its genus can exercise a tyrannical exclusivism all of its own. Its main weapon is manipulation of the spoken word, the more abstruse, pretentious, incomprehensible, and recondite, the better. The "snowing" of others to prove one's own intellectual superiority means being able to talk about everything with great assurance and to drown one's opponent in quotations, facts, and namedropping. Intellectual exclusivism is reinforced by the existence of "les grandes écoles," emergence from whose hallowed halls guarantees great prestige and often a viselike hold on the best jobs. Entrance by stiff competition only, please. The crème de la crème are the graduates of Normale Sup, l'ÉNA and l'X.

The ultimate intellectual hothouse is l'École Normale Supérieure, where the likes of Sartre, Malraux, and de Beauvoir, **"ont usé leurs fonds de culottes"** (wore out the seats of their trousers; that is, went to school). The end product is a **"normalien,"** and there ain't nothin' normal about those characters.

Know an **"énarque"**? He/she is a product of the highly competitive, postgraduate École Nationale d'Administration, a supertechnocrat with highly developed skills in the art of analyzing and dissecting (and not necessarily constructing) with tremendous command of language. He/she is destined for the high ranks of government service and is a readily identifiable, self-confident character.

What's the X? More reverence, please, l'X being not an unknown quantity but the very selective (intellectually speaking) École Polytechnique for engineering. Don't be put off by the polytechnic business; this is no second-class institution. One emerges with a passport to the upper reaches of the business world, full of theory and perhaps less so of practical knowledge, but that precious piece of paper precludes querying of one's ability. A **"polytechnicien"** makes a good marriage catch, as his earning power is pretty well guaranteed, unlike the aforementioned, whose involvement with the meaning of life, art and literature, or government service may not necessarily be rewarded in financial terms.

PROVINCIAL BRETHREN

Leaving Paris, what of the provincial brethren? Beyond the stereotype of the lumpen-provincial, there are regional variations: the "Marseillais" are considered liars and thieves, the "Corses" (Corsicans) lazy loudmouths, the "Alsaciens" Teutonic "bouffeurs de choucroûte" (sauerkraut-eaters), the "Basques" impetuous, and the "Bretons" thick.

The following commonly used expressions make use of certain accepted images:

faire une promesse de Gascon	to make an empty, vain promise
une histoire marseillaise	a tall story
répondre en normand	to answer evasively, non-committally
un(e) cousin(e) à la mode de Bretagne	a very distant cousin

A word on the "Normands": inhabitants of a rich, agricultural province noted for its butter, cream, and cheese, they are known particularly for their love of rich food. To help ingest gargantuan meals, rather than vomit "à la romaine," they devised **"le trou normand"** (the Norman hole). In the middle of a meal, one is given a glass of Calvados, the searing, local apple-based spirit whose function is to burn away previously downed dishes, thereby leaving more room—the "hole" in which to shove more food.

100

XIII
YOUR PH.D. EXAM

Armed with the knowledge gleaned from this book and from *MERDE!*, you must surely understand French better and more deeply than some jerkoff Ph.D. grind, so I have devised our own Ph.D. exam. Pass this one and, God forbid, you'll almost be a Frog! (Answers and translations on pages 103 and 104.)

PART A

"Les citations truquées" (falsified quotes). A few famous quotes have been tampered with. Where's the joke?

1. Je bande donc je suis. (René Descartes)

2. Le faim justifie les moyens. (Friedrich Nietzsche)

3. *Don Diègue*: Rodrigue, as-tu du coeur?
    Rodrigue: Non, j'ai du pique. (Pierre Corneille)

4. L'enfer, c'est les Parigots. (Jean-Paul Sartre)

PART B

Translate:

1. La reine Victoria: j'sais pas si son prince boche, Albert, était monté comme un âne mais, en tout cas, elle et lui, c'était du vrai lapinisme! Mais quand son Bébert a passé l'arme à gauche, elle en a eu gros sur la patate, elle a pleuré comme un veau et après, le zizi, c'était zéro pour la question. Ça s'appelle l'ère victorienne: "Le sexe? Nous, on est pas amusés!"

2. L'étranger de Camus est un drôle de zèbre. Sa vieille claque, il s'en bat l'oeil, il fait avaler son bulletin de naissance à un bicot; même quand il va se faire raccourcir, il s'en fout du quart comme du tiers.

3. La Tchécoslovaquie tapait dans l'oeil d'Hitler; il n'y est pas allé avec le dos de la cuiller, il se l'est payée. Les alliés n'ont pas remué le petit doigt. Chamberlain est même allé faire du lèche-cul et est revenu avec la déclaration de Munich qui ne valait pas un pet de lapin et où Hitler faisait des promesses de Gascon. Malgré tout, quand il est entré en Pologne, la moutarde est montée dans le nez des alliés et la guerre fut déclarée.

4. Les Franchouillards ont l'art de faire tout un plat de mecs désastreux: regardez Louis XIV et Napo, tous deux des mégalos à caractère de chien. Ils ont ramené leur fraise dans les affaires des autres pays, mais leurs idées de grandeur ont tourné au vinaigre. Un type qui s'est bien démerdé quand même c'est cette girafe de Gaulle, le gégène intello qui, même quand la France était sur les genoux, a fait des pieds et des mains pour continuer son one-man-show à Londres.

5. L'URSS mal léché, c'est Kroutchev battant sa table avec sa godasse.

102

PART A

1. The original is "Je pense donc je suis." But this version shows even greater proof of one's being alive ("bander" = to have an erection).

2. The translation of Nietzsche's "The end justifies the means" uses the French "la fin," but no doubt its homophone "la faim" (hunger) is an equally valid motive for action.

3. This is a classic schooldays joke. In *Le Cid*, the old geezer Don Diègue is slapped across the face by the father of his son's (Rodrigue's) fiancée (Chimène). He thinks it's a big deal, and in the scene whence comes the authentic quotation, he is about to ask Rodrigue to kill Chimène's dad (Don Gomès). He asks Rodrigue if he's got guts, or balls, or whatever ("as-tu du coeur?"). At school, instead of Corneille's answer, we all used to scream out "Non, j'ai du pique!", a "clever" play on the words for card suits ("du coeur" = hearts, and "du pique" = spades).

4. Sartre thought that hell was other people ("les autres"), but a vision of a hell made up only of Parisians ("Parigots") is terrifying enough.

PART B

1. Queen Victoria: I don't know if her kraut prince, Albert, was well hung, but anyway the pair of them bred like rabbits! But when her Bertie kicked the bucket, she was heartbroken. She cried her eyes out and after that, no more screwing. It's what's called the Victorian era: "Sex? We are not amused!"

2. Camus's stranger is a weirdo. His mom kicks the bucket, he doesn't give a damn, he does in some wog; even when he's going to the guillotine, he couldn't care less.

3. Czechoslovakia caught Hitler's fancy; he wasn't subtle about it, he just helped himself to the place. The allies didn't lift a finger. Chamberlain even went off to kiss some ass and came back with the Munich declaration which wasn't worth the paper it was written on and in which Hitler made promises he had no intention of keeping. Nonetheless, when he went into Poland, the allies got hot under the collar and war was declared.

4. Froggies love making a big deal out of losers: take Louis XIV and Boney, both ill-tempered megalomaniacs. They stuck their noses in other countries' business but their grandiose ideas went sour on them. On the other hand, one fellow who managed to do quite well was that beanpole de Gaulle, the intellectual general who, even when France was on her knees, moved heaven and earth to continue his one-man-show in London.

5. "L'URSS mal léché" is a pun on "l'ours mal léché" (= an uncouth fellow; literally a badly licked bear) which applies to the world-famous scene in which Khrushchev banged his shoe on a table while making a point at the United Nations.